NEWSPEAK

a dictionary
of modern English

IAN WILKES

Illustrated by
ASH

D1741818

IAN HENRY PUBLICATIONS

ISBN 0 86025 537 9

Published simultaneously by
Ian Henry Publications, Ltd.
20 Park Drive, Romford, Essex RM1 4LH
and
Players Press, Inc.
P O Box 1132, Studio City, Calif 91614-0132
and printed by
L.P.P.S. Ltd.
128 Northampton Road, Wellingborough
Northamptonshire NN8 3PJ

Look hard (see page 32)

Control freak (see page 16)

INTRODUCTION

This compilation of over 600 words and phrases that have a tendency to confuse (deliberately in a number of cases) has a number of strands –

Slang - coming from a number of sources, *e.g.* sickies

Officialese - very often made up to inflate the presumed importance of a post, *e.g.* environmental hygienist

Jargon - the lazy way of offering a cliché rather than having to do some thinking, *e.g.* facilitator

Wordplay - it is unclear whether such words as 'affluenza' have been used except in jokes

Obscurantism - often using 'real' dictionary words, but wrapping them up so as to confuse: politicians and the National Health Service are particularly good at this, *e.g.* endogenous convergence

The Internet - a whole vocabulary of its own, which has only been touched on only lightly in this work, *e.g.* blog

Euphemisms - polite talk about mildly 'naughty' subjects, *e.g.* bathroom tissue

Deliberate misprints - bra-maid, featured in an article in the *Romford Recorder* 1 August, 2003

American imports - only those that have definitely crossed the Atlantic are included, *e.g.* Neo-cons

Unless it has been introduced unconsciously teenage slang has been excluded.

I have to admit that a number of entries in this volume have definitions of which I am unsure – ambiguity creeps in to a fair number of these words which may change their absolute meaning from usage to usage.

I would be pleased to accept suggestions as to more correct definitions of any of the entries in this work! And suggestions for words that I have not come across. Contact me via my publishers, please.

I have to thank a number of contributors, most of them inadvertent, to this compilation, including many government spin doctors, local government officers, journalists, advertising agencies and social service workers. Individuals who have fed me material are Eddie Maguire and Steve Crancher.

Although new examples of Newspeak surface in every day's newspapers, I thought I had broken the back of the collection until an article on the 'rubbish jobs' for which Gareth Walsh had applied in the previous four months appeared in the *Sunday Times* of 13th July, 2003. My thanks to Mr Walsh.

Ian Wilkes

A

Abled - as opposed to disabled

Ableism - discrimination in favour of the healthy

Acceptable - semi-popular aspects of an unpopular subject. "The acceptable face of capitalism."

Access co-ordinator - doorman

Access course - crammer. "If we're going to get Adrian into university he'll have to go on an intensive access course."

Action plan - local government-speak for talking rather than doing

Add-in - an extra function of a computer

Adhocracy - management team assembled to deal with a single, probably unusual, item

Affluenza - the infection of being well off

Affordable housing

- cheap(ish), often ratepayer-subsidised, housing. "It's a small awkward-shaped plot

with difficult access, so let's bung in some affordable housing to keep the Mayor happy."

Aga saga - country-based romantic novel

Aggro - disturbance

Air kissing *see* Mwah

Airport fiction - novel of many pages that can be discarded when a 'plane journey is completed, often without finishing the book

All-terrain bike - a machine that can go anywhere on two wheels

Alpha geek - the only one in the office who knows how to work the new computer

Ambient replenishment - shelf stacking in a supermarket

Ambulance chasers - solicitors who encourage individuals to claim the often unclaimable

Announcementitis - urge to make headlines

Anorak

- someone who pursues an interest to obsessional level. "Leslie spends all his spare

time on railway platforms collecting engine numbers. He's a right anorak."

Aquacise - exercises in shallow water

Arboricultural Officer - chap who knows about trees

As low as... - fairly cheap if you buy a roomful. "Carbon paper as low as two pence a sheet when you buy seventeen gross or more."

Aunty - British Broadcasting Corporation

At the end of the day - where the buck stops

At this point in time - now

Aurally challenged

- deaf

Awesome - expression of amazement. "That water chute was awesome."

Axis of Evil - countries that are perceived to threaten the American dream

B

Babe - pretty young woman
Baby-boomer - person born in the 1950s
Bad hair day

- twenty-four hours when nothing goes right

Balanced scorecards - a reasonable view of things

Bancassurance - the selling of services outside accepted banking operations by local branches

Band of resources - money. "We have a sufficient band of resources to finance the project to build a bridge from Cornwall to Brittany."

Barfly jumping - a 'sport' involving throwing oneself at a prepared vertical surface with suction pads or velcro stickers on hands and feet

Bargain - modest price for something you really didn't want anyway. "Save pounds on the bargain of the week – a multi-purpose carpet sweeper and coffee grinder."

Base jumping - throwing oneself off very tall buildings or cliffs with a parachute attached

Bathroom tissue - lavatory paper

Beeb - British Broadcasting Corporation

Been there, done that, got the T-shirt - to have done something thoroughly. "Rock-climbing? I've been there, done that, got the T-shirt. Never again!"

Behaviour management - keeping the kids quiet

Benchmarking - achieving an acceptable standard

Benchmarking a reclaimable workload in progress - backlog

Benefits package - perks of the job. "The position will attract a significant benefits package, including car, free parking, five weeks' holiday and luncheon vouchers."

Benefit tourism - travelling around to get maximum social security benefits

Best practice - doing things the accepted way rather than trying to be clever

Beverage - soft drink with pretensions

Bimbette - bimbo under the age of 14

Bimbo - young lady with more cleavage than brains

Binge drinking - drinking for drinking's sake

Biodiversity - all the various things found in the water and on the land

Bipolar disorder - manic depression

Black information - details about poor credit risks held by banks

Blaxploitation - manipulation of black interests

Blended learning - spending large sums of money to make sure that theory and practice broadly complement each other

Bling - flashy, show-off jewellery

Blog - personal internet site used as a diary, usually by journalists who want to write outside their usual remit

Blogging - spending inordinate time on the internet

Blue chip companies - big companies

Bluey - lightweight airmail letter, especially those used by overseas-based fighting personnel

Bodice-ripper - a historical novel or film that concentrates more on the female form than on the historical context. "I know the plot is rubbish, so take shots from above to get maximum cleavage."

Body double - a stand-in for a film actor or actress in nude scenes

Bog standard - as good as we're going to get in most schools or hospitals. "Kevin went to a bog-standard comprehensive and then could only get a job as a porter in a bog-standard hospital."

Bogof – 'buy one get one free' in shops

Boiler rooms - illegal call centres, mainly run by westerners in South-East Asia

Bonkbuster - novel with more seamy sex than plot

Booziefloozy – a young woman who drinks to get drunk

Born again - newly evangelised individuals. "I've seen the light and been born again."

Bottom up - grass roots, basic

Boy racer - a young motorist who has occasionally been known to exceed the speed limit

Bra-maid [*sic*] - lady employed to collect underclothing after hen nights in night clubs

Break - a holiday lasting either for a weekend or more than a fortnight. "You've had a couple of days in Bruges? That must have been a nice break. I've just got back from three and a half weeks in the Seychelles. That *was* a nice break."

Britpop - popular music originating in the British Isles

Brown field site - generally contaminated inner-city land

Browse - wander around on the internet

Built ons - extras

Bull bar – chromium steelwork put on the front of vehicles to give maximum killing power

Bungee jump

- to throw oneself off a height attached to a rubber rope that you hope is not going to allow you to hit bottom

Burning - transcribing data on to a disc

Business process reorganising - re-arranging the office for presumed greater efficiency

Buzz - word of mouth marketing

C

Cabinet - a small committee of Borough or County Councillors trying to pretend they are in charge

Canteen culture - perceived sex discrimination, particularly in the police force

Canyoning - launching oneself down a mountain stream and trusting to one's God

Capacity building - activities aimed at increasing the skills and knowledge of people to enable them to take leading roles

Cargo pants - ephemeral fashion item

Carjacking - stealing a car by threats to its occupant

Cascade - pass on information. "We need Sophie here to cascade to the work-force."

Cash poor, property rich [CPPR] - people who live in large houses, but have little fluid money

Cashback - banking system for relatively small amounts at the check-out tills of large supermarkets. "That'll be sixty-three pounds, nineteen pence. Got your card? Want any cashback?"

Catering services - waitresses

Celeb - b-picture starlet

Celebrity novel - rubbish fiction supposedly written by a b-list actress or model

Chick-lit - novels by aging young ladies, often in 'diary' form

Cleaning operative - char-lady

Chair - person in charge of a meeting of stool pigeons

Challenging financial position - facing bankruptcy

Change management agenda - new ideas in a company

Charm offensive - kissing babies at elections taken to the ultimate

Chelsea tractors - four wheel drive off-road vehicles used for school runs in the towns and suburbs

Cherry-pick - choose the best from a selection. "We've cherry-picked from the figures, so we shouldn't have any aggro at the annual meeting."

Chessex girls – Sloane Ranger females inspired by Essex fashion

Chinese walls - dealings within a company that are not communicated from one department to another "Under no circumstances could it have been a case of insider dealing as we have Chinese walls between the finance department and the editorial staff."

Chopsocky - film with oriental setting and lots of semi-controlled mayhem

Chuggers - short for Charity Muggers, *i.e.* people ostensibly working for charities who approach others in the street and try to sign them up to regular payments, partly at least to the companies who employ them rather than the charities on whose behalf they appear to be working

Circular file - waste bin. "I promise to keep your curriculum vitae in the circular file."

Civic amenity recycling unit – rubbish dump

Clamper - company or individual who immobilises a vehicle and releases it for an extortionate payment

Cleansing - the clearance of a group from a location. "We've cleansed our village of gypsies."

Clear blue water - the obvious difference between two political parties. "There's clear blue water between Labour and New Labour on war on the Axis of Evil."

Closed circuit television - blurred images of town centre hot spot. "Indistinct pictures of those thought to be responsible were caught on CCTV."

Communications officer - telephone operator

Community transport - buses subsidised by local ratepayers, rather than the government or private enterprise

Comper - person addicted to competitions. "Regardless of the odds against, he entered every chance he could to win three hundred pounds for life, a penthouse suite in Sunderland, or a holiday in Afghanistan."

Compressed working

- sitting around with nothing to do

Conflict situation – war. "We regret that a conflict situation pertains between Crambostan and ourselves."

Consensus building skills - ability to manage personnel

Console operators - check-out girls

Conspicuous compassion - proclaim to the world the depth of your feeling. "I always wear my poppy all through October to show that my heart is in the right place,"

Constructive dismissal - trying to get a person to resign by changing work description or surroundings

Continuing professional development - courses for teachers and accountants

Continuous service improvement - get better

Contract monitoring officer - overcomes cynicism among staff who believe they should be doing something more productive than monitoring their own work

Control freak - Someone who considers the answer most important, regardless of what the question might have been

Corporate social responsibility - a company on the make, but theoretically contributing to the public benefit

Corporate strategy - a company's way forward

Cottaging rights - privacy in public loos

Couch potato - someone who spends a great deal of time doing nothing, often in front of a television screen

Creation system - building toy

Cross-functional support - make sub-bosses talk to each other

Cruising - wandering around hoping to meet that certain someone. "I'm just cruising until I'm thirty, then I'll start looking for a bloke in earnest."

Crumblie

- decrepit senior citizen

Customer [on train] - Passenger

D

Darrobee factor - indicative. "Darrobee the right way to get this job done."

Dawn raid - unexpected bids on the stock exchange

Deep hanging out - lengthy research undertaken in a single location

Definition politics - internal fighting in a political party

Degraded fashion - lacking sufficient power. "Our locomotive has behaved in a degraded fashion and will consequently be three hours late in Edinburgh."

Democratize - do it the western way... or else

Denied loading - passengers left behind when aeroplanes are deliberately overbooked

Detectorist - a wielder of metal-sensitive electronic equipment

Development intervention - training that is done during the working day

Dictator - pejorative term for leader of country with which one does not agree; diluted to 'strong leader' if it is economically expedient to continue relations with the country concerned

Digestion support team - people who advise on healthy foods

Dingleberries - udders of animals

Dink - double income, no kids. "They are a dink couple."

Disarmament - large countries bullying small countries into giving up their weapons

Distopia - opposite of Utopia

Distraction burglars - people who keep a person occupied on the front doorstep, while an accomplice makes entry via the back door

Diversity co-ordinator - settles disputes between white and non-white staff

Do one - exit fast. "Grab the ring and do one."

Domestics - Trouble in the home. "Poor old Sarg has been called out to three domestics this week already."

Domestic Violence Co-ordinator – a local government official who does not encourage, but tries to stop, disharmony in the home

Done and dusted

- completed. "That job is done and dusted."

Double whammy - tax that catches one coming and going

Downdating - going out with a social inferior

Downloaded - retrieved material from a computer

Downshift - leaving the rat-race for a more simple and relaxed lifestyle

Downsizing - moving to a smaller house

Drafting suggestions - changing facts into fiction

Dressing down - sloppy clothes in the office, generally on Fridays

Drive-by - a random shooting carried out from a car, generally on people not known to the perpetrator

Drop dead gorgeous - quite a nice looking female person

Drug abuse - over-dependence on drugs

Dumbing down - giving teachers a narrower vision, so that demands of future voters are restricted, making things simple for politicians

E

Eat my shorts (pants) - dismissive phrase. "Get lost! Eat my shorts, sunshine!"

Educational facilitator - teacher

Embed - get together

Employer placement - job (mainly for school children)

Empower – allow. "We train people to empower them to volunteer."

Enabling officer - Council worker who can move between disciplines

Endogenous convergence - a coming together naturally, as the Pound Sterling, the Euro and the Dollar

Engagement manager - someone to talk to someone

Environmenal hygienist - road sweeper

Equality officer - encourages disabled, black and other minority workers into higher positions

Equity release - putting your children's inheritance in hock by re-mortgaging your house at a knock-down rate to release 'capital'.

Essex girl - unintelligent bimbo [a phrase much resented by young ladies from Essex]

Estuary English - popular speech used in the area between London and Southend-on-Sea. The very funny dictionary to assist you with the lingo is *Dijja wanna say sumfing?* by Steve Crancher

Ethnic cleansing - clearing an area of an unacceptable minority

Euro - currency replacing the Deutschmark over most of continental Europe

Extended warranties - a device for making purchasers pay extra for makers' guarantees on products, particularly electrical goods

External clients - out-patients

External Relations Department - Public Relations Department

Extra-virgin

- the first pressing (and therefore purest) of a season's olives

F

Facilitation and presentation skills - can communicate. "Facilitation and presentation skills are essential for a dentist's receptionist."

Facilitator - Go-between

Facilitated - run by. "The morning networking will be facilitated by Miss Amabel Golightly."

Fair few - quite a lot. "There will be a fair few showers in the north-west tomorrow."

Fantasy football - gambling on imaginary teams put together by the competitor

Farewellers - those who check that pilferage has not been carried out by customers leaving DIY supermarkets

Fat cat - individual who is money-bloated

Fathers' worker - helps single fathers in their activities

Fatwa - ruling given by an Islamic cleric

Feel good factor - well being in people. "The most important part of the presentation is to emphasise the feel good factor"

Fingertip search - police fumbling for clues on the ground

Fit - Framework for internal transformation. Psychology designed to alter adults' lives without changing them directly

Five-a-day co-ordinator - individual who is paid to ensure that disadvantaged communities eat - and/or school meals include - not less than five vegetables or fruits

Fixedline voice - can talk on the telephone

Flame - electronic message on the internet calculated to annoy

Flash mobbing - a crowd organised over the internet descending on a location, acting in a friendly fashion, and then disappearing within a couple of minutes

Flatline - to die. "Fred was rushed into hospital with a heart attack, but he went flatline before they got him off the trolley."

Flexible hours - work time arranged to suit the convenience of the workers. "I know I'm late this morning, but I promise to work late tomorrow."

Float your boat - Agree. "That idea doesn't float my boat."

Fluologist - chimney sweep

Flying bishop

Anglican bishop who operates in another's diocese to minister to churches that do not agree with women priests

Folically challenged - bald

Foodie - liker of food

Footprint - the area covered by a development

Free gift - a come-hither whose hidden price is included in the cost of the main item

Free up - release [money or space]

Freebies - gifts that are (apparently) not charged for

Frontline – of immediate importance

Fruitloop - someone who is mentally deranged

Full Monty - the complete article: very often used to describe a male strip to the buff

G

Gap year - fourteen months between school exam results and doing anything.

Gastropubs – Public houses where food is more important than drink

Gay scene - a noticeably un-amusing environment

Geek - an eccentric person who specialises in something that few other people can be bothered to understand

Gesture politics - politics where style is more important than substance →

Gimpy - brash

Glass ceiling - unwritten bar to (generally female) advancement in a job

Go dark - a cut-back in television advertising

Golden parachute - pay-off for a director who loses his job, especially after a merger or a take-over

Google - look up on an internet search engine details about an individual

Gopher – an unimportant member of a managerial set. "On our team we use Andrew as a gopher to run messages and such."

Goss - gossip

Graduate calibre - non-university employee with potential. "He didn't go to university, but as he's the boss's son we regard him as of graduate calibre."

Graduate contribution scheme - top-up fees for university students

Graffiti - scrawls on walls, often restricted to the artist's initials or *nom de graffiti*. Very occasionally witty

Grandstanding - making much of yourself

Grazing - eating or drinking items taken off the shelves of a supermarket before reaching the till. "Little Wayne grazed his way through three bags of crisps and a bottle of cola before the checkout. Little rascal, isn't he?"

Greeters - individuals who welcome customers to DIY supermarkets

Grey gamer - elderly player of computer games

H

Hacked off - Very cross. "Tony was extremely hacked off and he left Peter in no doubt how angry he was."

Hacker - someone chained to a computer for enjoyment

HandyVan - service providing anti-burglar devices for the elderly (01255 473999)

Happy-clappy - Christian evangelists who celebrate religion in rhythm. "The funeral was happy-clappy. The only person not joining in was in the box."

Hawks and doves - aggressive and non-aggressive politicians

Head case

- someone who is unpredictable, possibly violently so

Heading up - leading. "Charles is heading up the Hospital Trust Board of Administrators."

Health outcome - NHS-ese for recovery

Health tourism - shopping around to find a hospital - or a country - that can best treat your disease

Hearts and minds - to win the support of a community that might be alienated. "The Americans are winning the hearts and minds of ordinary Iraqis by bombing the hell out of them."

Helipad - flat roof

Helpline - a device for leaving people waiting on the telephone for the answer to a simple enquiry. "This is the doctor's help-line. If you want an appointment next month press One; if you want a repeat prescription press Two; if you want an appointment with a chiropodist press Three; if you need a medical certificate for work press Four; if you require urgent medical assistance replace the handset, lift it up again, and press nine nine nine."

Herdperson - shepherd

High-intensity conflict - big battle

High-tech - anything that is incomprehensible to ordinary mortals

High level backbone process - trying to persuade more staff to take 'voluntary' redundancy

Hike - substantial price rise. "They've hiked the price of their own dog food by over thirty percent."

Himbo - male bimbo

Hippy chic - a fashion oxymoron

Hissy fit - throwing a tantrum

Hit - a site visited on the internet. "Our Sherlock Holmes site has received over fifty hits in the past week."

Hole in the wall

- cash or information dispenser on the street

Home alone - child left in house or flat by its parents

Home shopping - purchasing items from the internet

Home stager - one who re-designs your home in preparation for potential house buyers

Horizon scanning - looking into a 25 year + future

Horlicks - to bungle or muddle. "Alastair made a right horlicks of that dossier."

Horsiculture - farmland given over to riding stables

Hotting - driving very fast in a (probably stolen) car

Househusband - man with harassed expression

HR professionals - personnel officers

Human capital – personnel

Human factors specialist - a balancer of demographic imperatives

Human Resources Department - Personnel Department

I

In kind contributions - time given by volunteers or donations of equipment: not money. "In calculating the grant, in kind contributions can be costed and included as match funding."

In the loop - being *au fait* with a situation

In your face - aggressive shouting

Inbound and outbound - inward and outward bound

Inclusion - the process by which individuals are made to join in whether they want to or not!

Individualised graduate tax – top-up fees for university students

Infrastructure - the balance of a community

Innovative - new

Insider dealing - using company knowledge of accounts or prospects (illegally) on the stock market

Intellectual capital - knowledge

Interface - link between computer and its operator

Internal transport manager - a gentleman who collects abandoned supermarket trollies

Interpersonal skills - communication

Interpersonal – friendly

Intifadah - Arab uprising or threat

Investigative journalism - dig the dirt whatever the price

Item - recognised as being a pair of romantic people. "Simon and Laura aren't living together yet, but they certainly are an item."

J

Joined up - cohesive. "We need to do a little joined-up thinking to amalgamate the public libraries and the rent departments."

Jollies - visits that take people away from their normal environment. "The Leader of the Council and the Chief Executive are off to a jollies in our twin town in Germany."

Jungle fever - lust between different races

Junk mail

- material that comes through the letter-box, benefiting printers more than the senders and certainly more than the receivers

K

Kecks - trousers

Key deliverables - essential services

Key driver - pushy chap

Key performance indicators - observable targets in performance

Key stage - educational hurdles for children

Kick-start - thrust to start or re-start a project

Kid kit

- paraphernalia for babies

Kit off - to remove clothing. "Do you want to get your kit off now, darling?"

KM (see Knowledge management)

Knowledge management - trying to get people to pool ideas

L

Ladies' night - raunchy entertainment for females, who probably are not ladies

Landmark headquarters - over-ostentatious head office

Lap dancing - social therapy for tired businessmen

Larging it up - increasing the importance of an incident. "The police larged it up from a brawl into a riot."

Lateral thinking - looking at things from all angles

Latte - very frothy milky coffee

Learning and development co-ordinator - helps health workers to understand how to achieve government targets

Learning difficulty - Non-comprehension

Life manager - someone who does shopping and general organisation for those too busy to lead a normal life of their own

Life-limiting condition - terminally ill

Lipflaps - apparently off the cuff remarks. "Peter has generated so many lipflaps one now has to assume he plans it that way."

Listen up - listen

Literary hour - reading time in primary schools aimed at improving standards of barely literate children

Little number - lady's dress. "Oh, yes, I picked up this little number at that nice shop in Bruton Street."

Look hard - appear uncompromising

Lump - to make a successful swipe at a ball in cricket

Luvvies - chorus boys and girls

M

Make over - re-decorate

Mao chic - sophisticated Chinese gear

Making the muck - mix cement

Match funding - a percentage of a grant from a funding organisation that has to be found in cash or kind by the recipient of the money

Measure outcomes - exam results

Meet up with - meet (a thankfully rare double tautology)

Mega - very large indeed

Megaphone diplomacy - he who shouts loudest wins the argument

Members' Audience Co-ordinator - box office manager

Mentally challenged - stupid. "Tracey is mentally challenged when it comes to balancing her till receipts."

Meter maid - female traffic warden

Mezzanine debt - money owed to another party for which you are responsible. "The pub group has £198 million of mezzanine debt."

Middle donor - someone who gives a modest amount to a cause

Miff - mild annoyance. "I was miffed when my wife ran off with my best friend. Gee, I miss him!"

Migratory frames - illegal immigrants

Milestones - targets for achievement

Mindset - understanding

Mini recycling unit - single bottle bank

Mission creep - one thing leads to another

Mission statement - business plan

Mockney - assumed Cockney accent. "When he likes Tony can range from posh to Mockney in the course of one sentence."

Moneyback - a dividend on credit and purchases

Mooning - exposing one's buttocks as a gesture of contempt or, maybe, humourously

Mother of all [problems] – big! and how! "This promises to be the mother of all battles."

Mouse potato - a person who spends a great deal of time playing with a computer

Mouseholing - military entering a house by a break in the wall, rather than by a, possibly, booby-trapped door

Move the goalposts

- to alter circumstances during negotiations. "My bank keeps moving the goalposts so that I am always in its debt."

Movers and shakers - active people

Ms - adult female of uncertain marital status. "My vet says that he calls a virgin cat 'Miss', a mother cat 'Mrs', and a neutered cat 'Ms'."

Mug shot

- photograph portrait, especially in a prison environment

Mule - a mug carrying illegal drugs. "We've lost three mules in the last month, but there's plenty more where they came from."

Multimedia - using video, audio and still images to create an effect

Multiplex - cluster of small cinemas

Mung - potter about aimlessly. "I'm just going to mung around today."

Muppet - derogatory term for a young person

Mwah - an audible kiss noise made when ladies place their cheeks against each other

N

Naff - in the worst possible taste. "That dress is absolutely naff!"

Nanny state – the idea that 'they' will look after you from pre-cradle to post-cremation

Neo-Cons - American ultra-right wing politicians

Networking - trying to learn business rivals' trade secrets in a social setting

New initiative - doing something after being inactive for a number of years

Ngos - non-governmental organisations

Norties - the years between 2001 and 2010. "We were born in the 'seventies, but now we're living in the 'norties."

Not for profit organisation - voluntary body that ploughs any surpluses back into the concern

Nouvelle cuisine - food arranged on a plate for appearance and taste rather than quantity. "After Nigel and I had this nouvelle cuisine in that new place we went for a Chinkey."

Numeracy hour - desperate bid in junior schools to get children to a half-acceptable standard of mathematics

O

Of - have. "We couldn't of got that far in Europe wivout Beckham."

Offshoring – large corporations transferring simple banking or telephone answering jobs to India or China to avoid paying the British minimum wage

Ohnosecond - the billionth of a second after a wrong computer key has been pressed and a morning's work has been wiped out

One stop shops - an office where individuals who don't know the answers can pass you on to the person you should have spoken to in the first place. "The Council has a one stop shop a hundred yards from the Town Hall."

Only - as high as can be charged and hope to get away with! "Bargain holiday to Bognor! Only £103 per night per person."

Oracy - talking and listening. "Children shall be seen and heard."

Out - reveal that a person is a homosexual. "Peter has been outed by the media."

Out take - mistake by actor recorded on film

Outcomes Programme Coordinator - *unknown*, but Charities Evaluation Services employs one!

Outplacement – attempt by employer to find a job for an employee who has been released

Output - production of goods

Outreach - external

Outsourcing - get goods or parts from an outside organisation

Oxymoron - contradiction in terms. "To describe a one stop shop as efficient is generally an oxymoron."

P

Page Three girl - young lady with full mammary development. "My little Tracey is only seven, but she says she wants to be a Page Three girl when she gets a bit bigger."

Palm pilot - hand-held computer keyboard

Partner - male or female of uncertain marital status

Party pooper

- The first one to leave a social gathering to go home or be sick

Pashmina - ephemeral fashion item

Passenger Transport Exchange - Bus Station

Past the sell-by date - someone well over the top. "I like that Martin, but he's knocking thirty-five and getting past his sell-by date."

Peacenik - a proponent of peace at any price, who is prepared to go to war to defend this principle

Performance indicators - good or bad signs

Performance poetry - declaiming verse in a pub setting

Perp-walked – arrested

Pester power - nagging by children for parents to buy goodies advertised on television

PFI - private finance initiative. Expensive private mortgages for public buildings

Pillock - idiot

Pink pound – the perceived buying power of homosexuals as a group

Plantperson – nursery-man →

Plastic - credit cards

Plastic chicken - frozen chicken that has been pumped full of water and tastes more of the water than the chicken

Pleb - prole

PLWAs - African people living with Aids
Pole dancing

– a young lady lasciviously cavorting around an ornamental feature. "Phew, did you see that Jasmine pole dancing at the club last night?" [our artist is more innocent than believed possible]

Politically correct - defer cravenly to what is perceived as the right thing to say or think. "I can't tell you what I think about Channel Islanders as it is not politically correct."

Postholder

- employee

Postperson - deliverer of letters

Power dressing - clothing that shows how efficient you are

Prairie chic - lady from the American mid-west who can struggle into size 16

Pre-book – reserve or book [prefix entirely superfluous]. "Has sir pre-booked a table with us this evening?"

Pre-emptive strike - bash the other fellow first

Previous - a criminal record. "This man has got previous."

Primary casualty reception facility - hospital ship. "We've bombed all the local hospitals, so it's quicker to get a wounded man to a primary casualty reception facility at sea than helicopter him to care abroad."

Prime time - when television or radio companies think they can charge advertisers the highest prices

Priority area - location deemed to be in need of financial assistance

Progress your career - advance your career

Progressive governance – ever more control

Protected learning time facilitator - organiser of shut-downs so that staff can attend training sessions

Prole - pleb

Public sex environment - night club with lap dancing

Punk chic - young lady with tattoos and body piercing, but not wearing denim

Pupil-orientated experience - friendly classroom

Push factors - deadlines

Push the envelope - extend one's boundaries. "Stop doing that, Marcus. Don't push your envelope."

Pyjama game - cricket played in baggy costumes

Q

Quality assurance - getting things done by companies beholden to petty officials rather than searching for the best

Quality time - hours spent doing what you enjoy doing

R

Ram raid

- breaking through the front of a premises, often with a stolen four wheel drive vehicle

Rave - a gathering of people to participate in a hop happening

Reality television - live television, generally of people who will be hugely embarrassed when it is repeated

Re-arranging the deck-chairs on the *Titanic* - doing an absolutely useless task. "Changing the window display to bring in extra customers to our corner shop is like re-arranging the deck-chairs on the *Titanic*."

Recycling - totting

Redundant - sacked

Refuse collector - bin man

Regenerate - replace grass and shrubs with concrete and Victorian-style street furniture

Regime change - topple individuals who do not agree with American foreign policy

Resilience forum - civil defence

Re-skill - to train people into new technology

Resource packs - collection of leaflets in a folder

Resource procurement - fund raising

Retail outlet - shop

Retail therapy

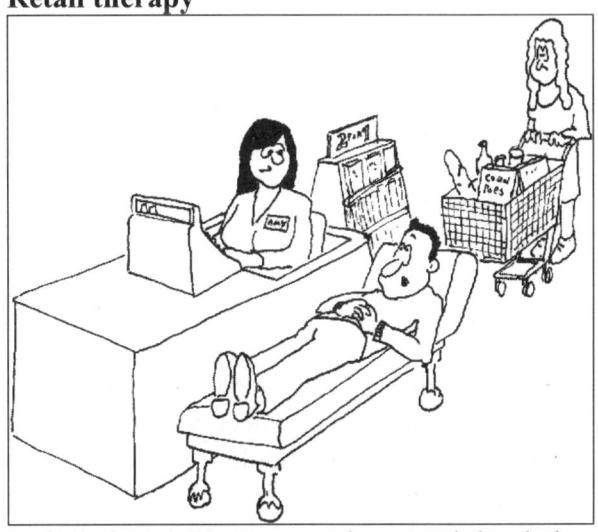

- shopping. "I was so depressed by being stuck at home that I had to pop out and do some retail therapy."

Return on investment - getting value on capital

Ring fence - to place constraints around allocated monies

Risk assessment - insurer

Road rage - to be annoyed by a fellow vehicle driver

Roadmap - strategic plan for international interference in national difficulties

Rocket science - very clever. Normally used in the negative for a straightforward task. "You're making a meal of that, squire. 'Struth, it's not exactly rocket science, is it?"

Rodent operative - rat catcher

Rogue state - any second-class nation that disagrees with American foreign policy

Rogue trader

- an individual who speculates and loses. "If Roger had brought it off, he wouldn't be a rogue trader, but a millionaire."

Rollover - postponed winnings. "There are no winners in this week's lottery, so the rollover for next week will be five million pounds."

Route one - football played mostly by long punts at goal

Ruff yoga - yoga for dogs and their owners

S

Safari party - a moveable dinner that starts in one house with the nibbles, moves on to another for the soup, and on and on, until nightcaps in the early hours (though where all the locations are, including the supposed hosts, few are certain). "Sorry to get you up, squire, but aren't you doing the pudding for Mike's safari party?"

Safe haven - area in a country where minorities are protected

Safe sex

- nookie protected from transmitted disease

Same sex lifestyle partner - chum

Sandwich generation - people bringing up a family and caring for elderly relatives at the same time

Sat nav - satellite navigation [in cars]

Save - spend fractionally less than advertised price on something you don't want. "Save over thirty pence by buying our new paint remover today."

Scam - illegal way of moving money from one individual to another

Scratch cards - gambling by removing the surface of a printed card to reveal a (possibly winning) symbol underneath

Script kiddy - juvenile with the ability to hack into computers and/or invent viruses

Secret shopper - undercover investigator of retail or service outlet. "We wanted to find out if the Housing Department was giving good advice, so we sent in a secret shopper."

Security - paranoia surrounding American politicians

Semi-fast train - slow train

Semi-permissive - the uneasy peace that follows a war and that results in an occupying force

Senior moments - flash of forgetfulness in the aging. "That Anne Robinson asked me what was the capital of France and I had a senior moment."

Service user - anyone who gets Council help free-ish

Set aside - agricultural land taken out of the production chain

Shades - Sunglasses

Shock-jock

- a person who deliberately sets out to upset his or her audience

Shop-putting - a practical joke involving bringing items into a shop and leaving them on the shelves to confuse people on the check-out when the item is taken out

Shopmobility co-ordinator - organises wheel-chairs for crumblies

Short-termism - live for the day

Sickies - doctors' notes excusing a person from work

SIF - single issue fanatic. The worst sort of person to have on a general committee, where he will repeat his obsession at length at every opportunity: either his or her fixation is solved

– whereon he leaves the committee - or it isn't
– whereon he leaves the committee

Signposting - directing

Silver spenders - mature people frittering their pensions

Silver surfers - retired people who spend their time on the internet

Single regeneration budget - government funding to boost local areas

Singleton - person with no partner

Skills development - apprenticeship

Skivvies - boxer shorts

Sleasebag - a person who is not ethical in his or her dealings

Smart card - credit card a bit above itself

Smoothing - official-speak for the rounding up of prices following the conversion of national currencies to the euro

Snail mail

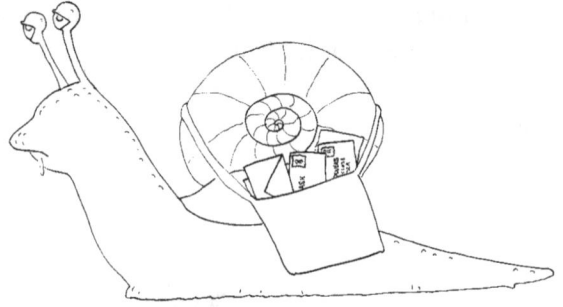

- very second class post

Social cleansing - removing groups from an area

Social engineering - Juggling white/black, male/female, under and over educated

Social enterprises - organisations that are ethnically aware

Social exclusion - deprived communities that do not have decent housing or job opportunities

Social fences - low dividers of gardens, so that neighbours are forced to look at each other

Social inclusion - attempts to prevent Social exclusion (*q.v*)

Social justice - equality for a selected few

Solutions consultant - Information assistant

Sound bite - the only eight seconds in a politician's speech considered worth reporting

Sourcing funds - obtaining money for charities

Space hosts - those who direct cars to vacant lots in supermarket car parks

Spam - unwanted junk e-mails, often offering untold wealth arising from a complicated inheritance problem in Africa, which you are invited to underwrite illegally

Speed camera - a traffic calming measure that causes the motorist in front of you to brake sharply

Speed hump

- a traffic calming measure that pollutes the environment and plays merry hell with ambulances in a hurry

Spin - attempt to bury bad news

Spin-doctor

- an individual who manipulates news. "Health Service hospitals these days have more spin doctors than medical doctors."

Spinning - making bad news palatable

Spotted Richard - pudding in a pretentious restaurant

Spud - salutation by banging closed fist against closed fist

Squeegee man - person who cleans windscreens at traffic lights unsolicited and who then demands payment

Spread trading - there are entire books written on this one subject, which is barely understood by people outside the City!

SSSI - Area of scientific significance, protected unless it is needed for commercial development

Stabilise - feed. "We need to stabilise Zimbabwe."

Stakeholders - financially interested people

Stalker - person obsessed with another individual who pursues that individual unceasingly

Start up grant - donation to help new organisation

Starter home - one-bedroomed dolls' house

State of the art - the absolutely latest gimmick

Statementing - identifying a child as needing special attention

Steaming - a gang racing through a crowded area, often pick-pocketing on the way

Stranger danger - perceived threat to children from any or every outsider

Streamline - make redundancies and profit for shareholders

Step aerobics - physical exercise concentrating on walking up and down real or imaginary steps

Street art - graffiti with attitude

Strike action - a contradiction in terms (or, in newspeak, an 'oxymoron') - It really means inaction because of strike – except, of course, from a few 'union bosses' who have a higher profile and have to appear to work much harder when there is a strike than they do ordinarily

Stringent contact management - close supervision

Sub-cut - [medical] sub-cutaneous

Super-rich - People who have so much money that good taste doesn't come into it.

Suss - to be aware. "We sussed out the opposition."

Sysop - computer systems operative

T

Tag - graffiti artist's signature

Take away - When ordered over the telephone, a meal delivered to the wrong address

Targetitis - obsession with the making of achievements to reach

Task - authorise. "The police are tasked to put truants back into school."

Telecon - telephone conversation

Teleshopping →
- buying retail over the telephone

Tesco rural - out of town supermarkets designed to fit into an idyllic landscape grounded in thatched cottages and roses round the door

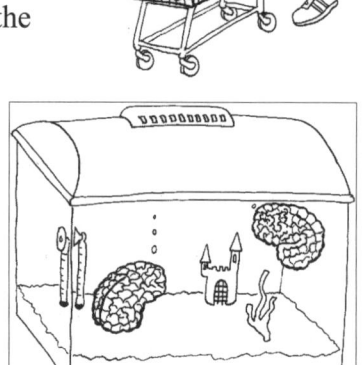

Think-tank →
- the innovative section of an organisation

Third sector - equates the plight of charity organisations with the third world

Thong - an item of feminine underwear calculated to bring tears to the eyes of both wearer and spectator

Three minute dating - instant courtship

Time-line - on schedule
Tired and emotional - drunk
TLC - tender loving care
To die for - must have. "She had the sort of figure to die for."
Toofers - two for the price of one offers
Top-down - instructions from a superior
Touchy-feely - contact of flesh rather than contact of mind
Toy boy - a youngish man kept by an older woman →

Trading down - taking a job below one's capabilities
Traffic calming - slowing down of vehicles
Tree hugger - enthusiastic environmental campaigner
Trolley dolly - air stewardess
Trolley rage - exasperation in a supermarket
Trophy wife - a bimbo married to a rich older man
24-7 people - on the go all the time
Twigloo - a tree house built by protestors to impede progress on a road scheme
Twilight merchandiser - evening shelf stacker
Twirlie - free-travel-pass user. "Oh, I know I can't use the bus before nine-thirty. Am I twirlie?"

U

Umbrella organisation - a larger body that speaks for a number of smaller groups

Unisex - remarkably, not a hairdresser devoted to a single sex, but one who styles for all sexes

Upsizing - moving to a residence larger than is necessary

Upwardly mobile - ambitious

Urban legend - remarkable things that have happened to the friend of a friend. "A friend told me about one of his mates picking up this hitch-hiking ghost."

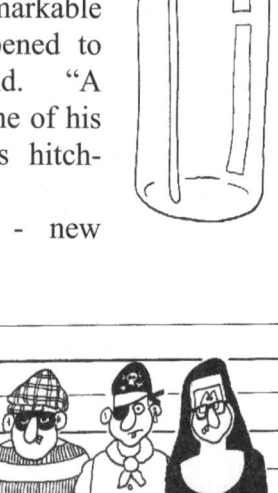

Urban regeneration - new houses

Usual suspects

- individuals who can be expected to rock the boat

V

Value meals - cheap prepared food
Vertically challenged - short
Viewrinals - video advertisements in gents' public conveniences
Viewloo - video advertisements for ladies to watch while queuing for a cubicle
Viral condition - belly ache or, maybe, hangover
Virgins - all owned by Richard Branson
Virtual reality - the sensation of 'walking' through a television screen
Vision - talking, rather than doing. "We have a vision of the Borough in the next century."
Visually challenged

- short sighted
Voice over - dub an existing film image, probably with different words. "The original was in French, so speak English with a French accent."

W

Walk about - a royal person, a senior politician or a pop star soils their shoe leather on tarmacadam. "Gorgeous George was mobbed when he attempted a walk about in Gateshead."

Walking officer - official paid to try to get children to walk to school

Wannabees

- aspirant Page Three girls

Waste management - bin men

Waste tourism - dumping rubbish on other people's property to avoid collection charges. "The Council charges for garden rubbish sacks, so we do a bit of waste tourism into the next street."

Weapons of mass destruction - threatening armaments that are alleged to be stockpiled by countries that do not agree with American foreign policy: often found in deserts, as are mirages...

Welfare rights advisor - person who ensures that a deprived area receives as many state benefits as can be managed

Well... - a word used by politicians and television journalists while they sort out in their minds what to say

Wheelie - person in a wheelchair. "To try to get a wheelie upstairs single-handed while still in his chair is hazardous."

White information - to establish whether a person is credit-worthy

White van man - potential cowboy

Wimp - unathletic to a degree

Window of opportunity - a spare couple of hours. "I seized a window of opportunity to replace the light bulb."

Wireperson - electrical fitter

WMD - *see* Weapons of mass destruction

Work experience - cheap labour. "We have sent the fifth form out on work experience potato-picking."

Workwear - uniform

World class - somewhere near average. "We are promoting a world class National Health Service."

Wuss - a wimp's wimp. "You're such a wuss; blimey, even my grandmother could abseil down Nelson's column."

Y

Yardie - member of a West Indian gang

Yellow 2 alert - red alert anywhere else than a new hospital (e.g. Worcester), which has been built with too few beds

Yips - muscular spasm when a golfer tries to put

Yob - a young gentleman about town with a tendency to break a beer glass into a friend's face

Yobette - a young lady who specialises in tearing other young ladies' hair

Z

Zero tolerance - no. "We have adopted zero tolerance to Councillors being drunk in the Town Hall."

Zoo radio

- rude broadcast talk show

APPENDIX

Many appointments, particularly in local government circles, may not be obscure to those placing the advertisement – but a small debate might be generated as to what precisely is the function of the people whose job advertisements all appeared in a single week in October 2003 –

Direct payment co-ordinator (Bexley Council)

Young people's co-ordinator (Derby City Council)

Overview & scrutiny officer (Milton Keynes Council)

System support manager (North Warwickshire Borough Council)

Corporate services director [six figure salary negotiable] (Nottingham City Council)

Strategic project manager (Rhondda Cynon Taf County Borough Council)

Team leader, neighbourhood road safety initiative (Tameside Council)

Strategy manager for innovation (North Staffordshire Regeneration Zone)

Income collection officer (East Thames Housing Group)

Fundraising database officer (Notting Hill Housing Group)

Senior resident participation consultant (The Housing Executive)

Supporting people review manager (The Housing Executive)

Data quality officer (Christie Hospital NHS Trust)

Promotion specialist, young people's sexual health (South West Kent Primary Care Tust)

Partnership co-ordinator (Norfolk County Council)

Portal development officer (Pendle Borough Council)

Distributed systems manager (University of Aberdeen)

... and four other job descriptions contributed in the same issue of the periodical by a confused Mr Caedmon Featherston of Seaton, Devon

14-19 pathfinder co-ordinator

Community learning co-ordinator

Development officer, accreditation of low-intensity direct access service

Child pedestrian skills training co-ordinator

... who suggests the last-named might be officialese for Lollypop Lady.

Mr Featherton enquires what do these people do that is of essential use?

Answers please, to the compiler of this gallimaufry of confusing words and phrases c/o The Publisher.

Twigloo (see page 55)